30 Days With The Lord:

A Living Christian Devotional

Spending Time Each Morning Connecting With God

This book isn't just another devotional; it's an invitation to spend unhurried and uninterrupted time with God. In the midst of life's chaos and distractions, it's easy to lose sight of our relationship with our Creator. Within these pages, you'll embark on a transformative journey —one that I hope will deepen your faith, strengthen your connection with God, and set the tone for each day in His presence.

Each morning holds the promise of a fresh start, a new opportunity to draw near to God and align your heart with His will. As you dive into these daily readings, you'll encounter the timeless truths of the Christian faith, breathing new life into your spiritual walk. From inspirational guidance to related Bible Verses, each page is carefully crafted to guide you into a deeper understanding of God's love and purpose for your life.

But this devotional isn't just about reading words; it's about experiencing God's presence in a tangible way. It challenges you to set aside the rush of daily life and carve out quiet moments to spend time each day with Jesus. Through reading, reflecting and applying, you'll develop a more meaningful and intimate relationship with God—one that infiltrates every aspect of your life.

Whether you're seeking a spiritual renewal, guidance in your daily challenges, or simply a deeper connection with God, this devotional is here to walk alongside you on your journey of faith. It's a compass for your walk, pointing you towards the blessed life that Jesus promised. Each day offers a new opportunity to encounter the transformative power of God's grace and to walk in His truth.

So, are you ready to embark on this Christian journey? Set aside the distractions, quiet your heart, and allow God's presence to fill your mornings with peace, joy, and purpose. Let this devotional be the catalyst for spiritual growth and renewal in your life—a journey towards deeper intimacy with the One who loves you beyond measure. Your time with God awaits—let's begin this journey together!

Table of Contents

Introduction

"I lift up my eyes to the hills—where does my help come from? My help comes from the Lord, the Maker of heaven and earth."

Psalm 121:1-2

Welcome to this 30-day devotional journey! I am excited to share these daily reflections and prayers with you, and I hope they become a valuable part of your daily routine, drawing you closer to God each day. This devotional was born out of a deep desire to connect with God in the quiet moments of life, and I believe it can help you find that same peace and closeness.

Each morning, I love to sit on my front porch, drinking my coffee and spending quiet time with God. This practice has been a source of great comfort and inspiration for me, and it's something I inherited from my father. My father was a man of deep faith, and he had a tradition of sitting on his front porch each morning, overlooking the hills of Central Texas. He would sip his coffee and find solace in the quiet and in the beauty of God's creation.

Before he passed away, he shared with me his favorite verse, Psalm 121:1-2: "I lift up my eyes to the hills—where does my help come from? My help comes from the Lord, the Maker of heaven and earth." This verse reminded him of the hills he looked upon each morning and served as a constant reminder of God's ever-present help and strength. It's a memory that I hold dear and a practice that I continue to this day.

This devotional is designed to be a part of your quiet time each morning with God. Just as my father and I found peace and strength in those early morning moments, I hope you will too. Each day's reflection is paired with a prayer and a topic meant to guide you through various aspects of faith and life. Whether you're dealing with uncertainty, finding gratitude, or seeking God's guidance, these devotionals are here to support you on your journey.

Imagine starting your day with a warm cup of coffee, your Bible, and this devotional. Settle into a comfortable spot, maybe your own front porch or a favorite chair, and let the quietness find you. Begin by reading each day's devotional, reflect on its message, and then spend time in prayer. Allow yourself to be open to God's presence and listen for His voice. This time can transform your entire day, setting a tone of peace, gratitude, and purpose.

In our busy lives, it's easy to get caught up in the whirlwind of daily tasks and forget to take a moment to breathe and connect with God. This devotional offers a structured way to carve out that time, ensuring that each day begins with a focus on what truly matters. The topics covered over these 30 days are meant to inspire and challenge you, helping you grow in your faith and deepen your relationship with the Lord.

Through this devotional, I hope to share the joy and comfort that comes from spending regular time with God. Whether you are just beginning your faith journey or have been walking with God for many years, these reflections are crafted to meet you where you are and to encourage you along the way.

As you embark on this 30-day journey, I pray that you will experience the profound peace and joy that comes from a closer walk with God. May each day's reflection and prayer be a source of inspiration and strength, drawing you nearer to the heart of the One who loves you unconditionally.

Thank you for allowing me to be a part of your faith journey. May this devotional become a treasured part of your daily routine, bringing you ever closer to God.

In loving memory of my father, Jim Jackson.

Day 1

TRUSTING GOD TO NAVIGATE

In the journey of life, entrusting our path to God is like handing over the steering wheel to the most skilled driver. It's about acknowledging that we may not have all the answers, but there's a divine guidance that surpasses our understanding. Letting God navigate our lives means finding solace in His wisdom, trusting that even in uncertain twists and turns, there's a purpose and a destination beyond our immediate sight. It's a profound act of faith, allowing God's love to be the compass that directs our steps, leading us toward a fulfilling and purposeful existence.

PRAYER

Dear Lord, help me trust You to guide my path each day. When I am faced with uncertainty or fear, remind me that You are my compass, leading me toward Your perfect plan. Give me the faith to follow Your direction, even when I don't see the whole road ahead. Help me to let go of my desire for control and to fully rely on Your wisdom and love. I trust that You are always with me, guiding me with Your hand. Strengthen my trust in Your guidance and help me to navigate life's journey with confidence in Your provision. In Jesus' name, Amen.

BIBLE VERSE

"Trust in the Lord with all your heart and lean not on your own understanding; in all your ways submit to him, and he will make your paths straight."

Proverbs 3:5-6

QUESTIONS TO REFLECT ON

1. What are some areas in your life where you find it difficult to trust God's guidance?
2. How can you remind yourself daily to rely on God's wisdom rather than your own understanding?

notes

_____

_____

_____

_____

_____

_____

_____

Day 2

LETTING GOD CHANGE YOU

Allow God to transform your life. Give Him the paintbrush to create a masterpiece out of the canvas of your existence. It's a willingness to let go of the past mistakes, regrets, and burdens, trusting that His love and grace can turn them into something beautiful. Just as a skilled artist sees potential in every stroke, God sees the potential for goodness and purpose in your life. Surrendering to His guidance means embracing a journey where His wisdom shapes your choices and His love molds your heart. Letting God change your life is an invitation to experience a transformation that goes beyond the surface, reaching deep into the core of who you are.

PRAYER

Father, I open my heart to You. Mold me and transform me according to Your will. Help me release my fears and embrace the changes You bring, trusting that Your plan is perfect. Change my heart and mind to align with Your purposes. Teach me to be patient in the process and to recognize Your work in my life. Grant me the courage to let go of the old and welcome the new with joy and faith. Make me more like Jesus each day, reflecting His love and grace to those around me. In Jesus' name, Amen.

BIBLE VERSE

"Do not conform to the pattern of this world, but be transformed by the renewing of your mind. Then you will be able to test and approve what God's will is—his good, pleasing and perfect will."
Romans 12:2

QUESTIONS TO REFLECT ON

1. What changes do you feel God is prompting you to make in your life right now?
2. How can you be more open to God's transformation in your heart and mind?

notes

_____

_____

_____

_____

_____

_____

_____

Day 3

FINDING GRATITUDE IN EACH MORNING

Gratitude should fill your heart each morning as you awaken, recognizing the precious gift of a new day. In the quiet moments before the hustle begins, you reflect on the simple yet profound blessing of being granted another sunrise. Life's uncertainties fade, replaced by the warmth of gratitude for the opportunity to embrace the challenges and joys that lie ahead. Each morning becomes a gentle reminder that, despite the struggles, you are entrusted with a fresh canvas to paint your journey, a chance to make a positive impact, and a reminder that blessings often arrive in the quiet moments of dawn.

PRAYER

Lord, thank You for the gift of a new day. Open my eyes to see Your blessings, big and small, and fill my heart with gratitude. As I wake each morning, help me to focus on Your goodness and the countless ways You show Your love. Let my first thoughts be of thanksgiving and praise for Your faithfulness. Guide me to carry this grateful spirit throughout the day, influencing my actions and interactions with others. May my life be a reflection of Your love and grace, always giving thanks for the new opportunities and mercies You provide. In Jesus' name, Amen.

BIBLE VERSE

"Because of the Lord's great love we are not consumed,
for his compassions never fail. They are new every morning; great is
your faithfulness."
Lamentations 3:22-23

QUESTIONS TO REFLECT ON

1. What are three things you can thank God for as you start
   your day?
2. How can cultivating a morning gratitude habit impact your
   attitude throughout the day?

notes

_____

_____

_____

_____

_____

_____

_____

God is Saying to you Today:

"I know you have a lot on your mind right now. Your family, your health, your finances, your career. It feels like the weight of the world is on your shoulders. My child, you are not alone. Give it all to me. I will make a way for you. I got this."

Day 4

LIFE'S CHANGES SHAPE US

God often allows the threads of challenging situations to weave through our days. These moments, though sometimes difficult, serve as opportunities for growth and transformation. Just as a blacksmith tempers iron through the fire, God uses life's trials to shape and refine our character. Embracing change becomes a journey of trusting in His wisdom, knowing that even in the midst of uncertainty, He is crafting a masterpiece out of the raw materials of our experiences. So, when situations stretch and mold us, let us lean on the understanding that God's plan is to shape us into stronger, wiser, and more compassionate individuals, ultimately guiding us toward a purposeful and fulfilling existence.

PRAYER

God, life is full of changes that can be challenging. Help me to see Your hand in every situation and trust that You are shaping me through each experience. Give me the strength to adapt and grow in faith, knowing that You use every change to mold me into Your image. When I face difficult transitions, remind me of Your constant presence and unchanging love. Teach me to embrace each new season with a hopeful heart and a willing spirit. Let my life be a testimony of Your transformative power and unfailing support. In Jesus' name, Amen.

"And we know that in all things God works for the good of those who love him, who have been called according to his purpose."
Romans 8:28

QUESTIONS TO REFLECT ON

1. How have past changes in your life shaped your faith and character?
2. How can you embrace current changes as opportunities for growth?

notes

_____

_____

_____

_____

_____

_____

_____

DISCOVERING YOUR WORTH

In the quiet moments of the morning, consider this profound truth:
God, the Creator of everything and the master of time, chose you.
It's not about your qualifications or flawless resume; it's about His
unwavering love and deliberate choice to embrace you. Imagine
being handpicked by the One who knows every star by name. You
are not an afterthought; you are a deliberate, cherished creation of
divine intention. In the grand story of existence, God's choice to
include you is a testament to your inherit worth. So, rest in the
assurance that you are not alone; you are chosen, held, and loved by
the Author of life.

PRAYER

Heavenly Father, remind me that my worth comes from You alone.
When I feel inadequate or unloved, help me remember that I am
fearfully and wonderfully made in Your image. Teach me to see
myself through Your eyes, full of value and purpose. Remove the
lies of the enemy that tell me I am not enough, and replace them
with Your truth. Help me to live confidently in the identity You
have given me, and to use my gifts for Your glory. Let me find my
worth and significance in being Your beloved child.
In Jesus' name, Amen.

"For he chose us in him before the creation of the world to be holy and blameless in his sight."
Ephesians 1:4

QUESTIONS TO REFLECT ON

1. In what ways do you struggle to see your worth as God sees it?
2. How can you daily remind yourself of your value in Christ?

notes

_____

_____

_____

_____

_____

_____

_____

Day 6

FINDING CONTENTMENT EVERYDAY

It's not about waiting for perfect circumstances or achieving all our goals; instead, it's an active choice to find joy in the present. Contentment flourishes in gratitude for small victories, shared laughter, and the warmth of the sun. While society often measures success in material wealth, a content heart values relationships, personal growth, and the ability to find joy in simplicity. Let go of comparison fueled by social media and celebrate your unique journey. In moments of discontent, practice gratitude, count your blessings, and acknowledge the lessons learned. Contentment is a state of mind that transforms ordinary moments into extraordinary experiences—embrace each day with gratitude, live in the present, and find profound joy in being content on the journey.

PRAYER

Lord, teach me to be content with what I have and where I am. Help me to find joy in the present moment and trust that You provide all I need. Show me how to appreciate the blessings that surround me, and to be grateful for each day. When I am tempted to compare myself to others or desire more than what You have given, remind me of Your perfect provision. Fill my heart with peace and satisfaction, knowing that You are my provider and You meet all my needs according to Your riches in glory. In Jesus' name, Amen.

BIBLE VERSE

"Keep your lives free from the love of money and be content with what you have, because God has said, "Never will I leave you; never will I forsake you.""
Hebrews 13:5

QUESTIONS TO REFLECT ON

1. What are some areas in your life where you struggle with contentment?
2. How can you practice contentment and gratitude today?

notes

_____

_____

_____

_____

_____

_____

_____

God is Active

Just because you can't see it, that doesn't mean God isn't active in your life. Thank Him for the times He saved you from what you didn't even know was trying to hurt you.

GOD GIVES US REST

In the hustle of our daily lives, it's easy to feel overwhelmed and drained. Yet, in the midst of chaos, we find solace in the promise that God generously offers us rest. Like a caring parent providing comfort to a tired child, God invites us to lay down our burdens and find peace in His presence. In those quiet moments, we discover a profound sense of renewal, knowing that we are not alone in our struggles. God's rest is not just a pause from our endeavors but a rejuvenating embrace that empowers us to face each day with strength and grace. As we seek refuge in His love, we find rest not only for our bodies but for our souls, finding comfort in the unending source of peace that God graciously provides.

PRAYER

Father, in the busyness of life, remind me to find rest in You. Help me to lay down my burdens and find peace in Your presence. Teach me to prioritize time with You, where my soul can be refreshed and renewed. When I am weary and overwhelmed, draw me to Your side where I can experience true rest. Restore my soul and renew my strength, knowing that You are my refuge and my strength. Let Your peace fill my heart and guide me through each day.
In Jesus' name, Amen.

BIBLE VERSE

"Come to me, all you who are weary and burdened, and I will give you rest. Take my yoke upon you and learn from me, for I am gentle and humble in heart, and you will find rest for your souls. For my yoke is easy and my burden is light."
Matthew 11:28-30

QUESTIONS TO REFLECT ON

1. How can you incorporate regular moments of rest into your busy schedule?
2. What are some practical ways that you can find rest in God's presence each and every day?

notes

GOD'S PLANS ARE BETTER

Sometimes we get so wrapped up in our own plans, thinking we know what's best for our lives. But God sees the bigger picture, the whole puzzle, while we're just looking at a few scattered pieces. Trusting in His plans means letting go of our own agendas and surrendering to His wisdom and love. Even when it doesn't make sense to us, His plans are always better than ours, leading us to places we never imagined and blessings we never expected. So, when things don't go our way, let's remember that God's got something better in store. We might not always understand it, but we need to learn to trust Him.

PRAYER

Lord, Your plans are higher than mine. When my plans fail, remind me to trust in Your perfect will. Help me to surrender my desires and follow the path You have set for me, knowing it leads to true fulfillment. Teach me to seek Your guidance in all my decisions and to trust that You know what is best for me. When I am tempted to go my own way, remind me of Your loving sovereignty. Help me to walk in faith, confident that Your plans for me are for good and not for harm, to give me a future and a hope. In Jesus' name, Amen.

BIBLE VERSE

"'For I know the plans I have for you,' declares the Lord, 'plans to prosper you and not to harm you, plans to give you hope and a future.'"
Jeremiah 29:11

QUESTIONS TO REFLECT ON

1. When have you experienced God's plans being better than your own plans?
2. How can you trust God's plan in areas where you currently feel uncertain or uneasy?

notes

FORGIVE LIKE GOD

Forgiving others the way God forgives us means letting go of grudges and extending grace even when it's hard. Just as God forgives us without keeping a record of wrongs, we should strive to forgive others wholeheartedly, releasing any bitterness or resentment. It's about showing compassion and understanding, knowing that we've been forgiven much ourselves. Even though, we haven't always deserved it, God has forgiven us of so much. We need to pay that forgiveness forward. By choosing to forgive as God does, we reflect His love and mercy in our relationships, fostering healing and reconciliation.

PRAYER

Father, help me to forgive others as You have forgiven me. Remove any bitterness from my heart and fill me with Your love and compassion. Teach me to extend grace and mercy, reflecting Your character in my actions. When I struggle with unforgiveness, remind me of the immense forgiveness You have given me through Jesus. Help me to release grudges and seek reconciliation, living in the freedom that Your forgiveness brings. Let my life be a testimony of Your grace, showing others the power of Your love.
In Jesus' name, Amen.

"Be kind and compassionate to one another, forgiving each other, just as in Christ God forgave you."
Ephesians 4:32

QUESTIONS TO REFLECT ON

1. Who do you need to forgive, and what steps can you take toward forgiveness?
2. How does remembering God's forgiveness help you to forgive others?

notes

_____

_____

_____

_____

_____

_____

_____

You Were on God's Wake Up List.

God woke you up today. You have purpose.
You have meaning. He woke you up again
because He has plans for you today. You
may not know what they are, but you need to
trust Him. Let Him lead you through today,
tomorrow and forever.

PRAYER CHANGES YOUR HEART

Prayer is like opening a window in your soul, letting in fresh air and light. When you pray, it's not just about asking for things or talking to God—it's also about listening and allowing Him to work within you. Over time, this practice softens your heart, helping you to see the world through a lens of love and compassion. As you pour out your worries, gratitude, and hopes, you find your perspective shifting. Your heart becomes more aligned with God's, making you more patient, kind, and understanding. Prayer doesn't always change your circumstances, but it always changes you.

PRAYER

Lord, draw me closer to You through prayer. As I spend time with You, change my heart and align it with Yours. Help me to see the world through Your eyes and respond with love and compassion. Teach me to pray with sincerity and faith, trusting that You hear and answer my prayers. Let my time with You transform my attitudes, thoughts, and actions. Fill me with Your peace and joy, and guide me to live out Your will each day. In Jesus' name, Amen.

"Do not be anxious about anything, but in every situation, by prayer and petition, with thanksgiving, present your requests to God."
Philippians 4:6

QUESTIONS TO REFLECT ON

1. How has prayer changed your perspective or attitude in the past?
2. What specific areas of your heart do you want God to change through prayer?

notes

_____

_____

_____

_____

_____

_____

_____

_____

Day 11

BLESSED, NOT LUCKY

Luck is a concept tied to chance, but as believers, we understand that our blessings come from God, not random chance. Instead of relying on luck, we trust in God's provision and guidance in our lives. Every good thing we have is a gift from Him, and it's important to acknowledge His hand in our blessings. When we recognize that we are blessed by God, we find peace and contentment knowing that His love and favor are upon us, guiding us through both the highs and lows of life. So, let's shift our focus from luck to recognizing and appreciating the abundant blessings bestowed upon us by our Heavenly Father.

PRAYER

Heavenly Father, remind me that my blessings come from You, not luck. Help me to recognize Your hand in every good thing in my life and give You thanks. Fill my heart with gratitude for Your constant provision and grace. Teach me to see Your blessings in both the big and small moments, and to always give You the glory. Let my life be a reflection of Your goodness and faithfulness. Help me to share my blessings with others and to be a living testimony of Your love. In Jesus' name, Amen.

BIBLE VERSE

"Every good and perfect gift is from above, coming down from the Father of the heavenly lights, who does not change like shifting shadows."
James 1:17

QUESTIONS TO REFLECT ON

1. What blessings in your life can you attribute to God's provision?
2. How can recognizing God's blessings change your outlook on your life?

notes

_____

_____

_____

_____

_____

_____

_____

GRATITUDE FOR UNSEEN BLESSINGS

Sometimes we forget to thank God for what didn't happen—the accidents avoided, the illnesses prevented, and the disasters averted. It's easy to focus on what's right in front of us, but we often miss the quiet blessings of protection and guidance. Let's take a moment today to be grateful for the unseen hands that have kept us safe and guided us away from trouble. Thank you, God, for protecting us from dangers we didn't even know about. These hidden blessings show us the constant care we often overlook but are so important. Let's appreciate and recognize these silent acts of kindness.

PRAYER

Lord, thank You for the blessings I cannot see. Open my eyes to Your work in my life and help me to trust in Your goodness even when I don't understand. Fill my heart with faith and gratitude for the ways You are moving behind the scenes. Teach me to be patient and to trust that You are always working for my good. Help me to remember that Your ways are higher than mine, and that You have a perfect plan for my life. Let my gratitude grow deeper each day as I reflect on Your unseen blessings. In Jesus' name, Amen.

BIBLE VERSE

"For he will command his angels concerning you to guard you in all your ways; they will lift you up in their hands, so that you will not strike your foot against a stone."
Psalm 91:11-12

QUESTIONS TO REFLECT ON

1. What are some blessings in your life that you often overlook?
2. How can you develop a habit of noticing and thanking God for unseen blessings?

notes

God Makes the Moves

God will remove you from a place where you used to be in order to save you from people and influences that are poisoning your mind against Him. He hears things you don't. He sees things you can't. He makes moves you won't. Let that sink in.

GIVE GOD ALL THE PIECES

As you start your day this morning, take a moment to sit quietly and spend some time with God. Imagine laying all the broken pieces of your life—your worries, regrets, and fears—at His feet. Trust that He is big enough to handle them and loves you enough to want to. In these quiet moments, feel His peace and reassurance. God doesn't need you to have everything together; He simply wants your heart, just as it is. Let His presence fill you with hope and strength for the day ahead, knowing that with Him, even the shattered parts of your life can be made whole again.

PRAYER

Father, I bring You all the pieces of my life. Help me to trust You with every part, knowing that You can make something beautiful from the brokenness. Guide me and heal me with Your love. Teach me to surrender my worries, fears, and doubts to You, trusting that You are in control. When I feel overwhelmed, remind me that You are my strength and my healer. Help me to rest in Your care and to find peace in Your promises. Let my life be a testament to Your power to restore and redeem. In Jesus' name, Amen.

"Why, my soul, are you downcast? Why so disturbed within me? Put your hope in God, for I will yet praise him, my Savior and my God."
Psalm 42:11

QUESTIONS TO REFLECT ON

1. What broken pieces of your life do you need to surrender to God?
2. How can trusting God with your brokenness lead to healing and peace?

notes

Day 14

BEGINNING THE DAY IN PRAYER

Starting your day with prayer is like setting a compass for your soul. In the quiet moments of the morning, before the busyness of life takes over, taking time to connect with God can fill you with peace, purpose, and perspective. It's a chance to express gratitude for a new day, seek guidance for the challenges ahead, and find strength in knowing you're not alone. Just a few minutes of heartfelt conversation with God can transform your outlook, grounding you in faith and preparing you to face whatever comes your way with grace and confidence.

PRAYER

Lord, I start this day with You. Guide my steps and fill me with Your Spirit. Help me to seek You first in all that I do, and grant me the wisdom and strength to follow Your lead. As I face the challenges of the day, remind me of Your presence and Your power. Fill my heart with Your peace and joy, and let Your love flow through me to those around me. Teach me to rely on You in every moment, trusting that You are with me every step of the way. In Jesus' name, Amen.

"Rejoice always, pray continually, give thanks in all circumstances; for this is God's will for you in Christ Jesus."
1 Thessalonians 5:16-18

QUESTIONS TO REFLECT ON

1. How can starting your day with prayer set a positive tone for the rest of your day?
2. What specific prayers do you want to include in your morning routine?

notes

COUNTING SIMPLE BLESSINGS

In our busy lives, it's easy to overlook the simple blessings that surround us each day. Whether it's the warmth of the morning sun, the laughter of a loved one, or even the comfort of a cozy bed, these small gifts are often taken for granted. But when we take a moment to pause and appreciate these everyday wonders, we find that gratitude fills our hearts with peace and joy. Let us remember to thank God for these simple pleasures, for they remind us of His constant love and care in every detail of our lives.

PRAYER

Father, help me to appreciate the simple blessings in life. Open my eyes to Your goodness in the small things and fill my heart with joy. Teach me to live with a spirit of gratitude each day, recognizing Your hand in every moment. When life feels overwhelming, remind me of the countless ways You show Your love and care. Help me to find joy in the ordinary and to celebrate Your faithfulness. Let my heart be continually filled with thanksgiving, and let my life reflect Your joy. In Jesus' name, Amen.

"Blessed is the man who remains steadfast under trial, for when he has stood the test he will receive the crown of life, which God has promised to those who love him."
James 1:12

QUESTIONS TO REFLECT ON

1. What simple blessings did you experience today that you can thank God for?
2. How can focusing on simple blessings change your perspective on life's challenges?

notes

_____

_____

_____

_____

_____

_____

_____

Give God the Pieces

Never doubt what God can do
with a broken life when you give
Him all the pieces.

Day 16

GOD IS OUR FIRM FOUNDATION

God is like the bedrock of our existence, the solid ground beneath our feet in a world full of shifting sands. When everything else feels uncertain and unstable, He remains steadfast and unchanging. Building our lives upon Him is like constructing a house on the firmest foundation, ensuring that no storm can shake its core. With God as our foundation, we can trust that we are rooted in something eternal and unbreakable, providing us with the strength and stability to weather any challenge that comes our way.

PRAYER

Lord, You are my rock and my foundation. When life feels shaky, remind me to stand firm in Your promises. Strengthen my faith and help me to rely on Your unchanging love. Teach me to build my life on Your truth, so that I can withstand any storm. When I face trials and uncertainties, remind me that You are my steadfast anchor. Fill me with Your peace and confidence, knowing that You are always with me. Let my faith in You be unshakable, and let my life reflect Your stability and strength. In Jesus' name, Amen.

BIBLE VERSE

"The rain came down, the streams rose, and the winds blew and beat against that house; yet it did not fall, because it had its foundation on the rock."
Matthew 7:25

QUESTIONS TO REFLECT ON

1. In what areas of your life do you need to rely more on God's strength?
2. How can you build a stronger foundation of faith in your daily life?

notes

_____

_____

_____

_____

_____

_____

_____

_____

Day 17

LET GO, LET GOD

Sometimes, life throws curveballs, and we feel like we're juggling too much. But here's the thing: we don't have to carry the weight alone. Letting God take the wheel isn't just a catchy phrase; it's an invitation to let go of our worries and trust that there's a bigger plan at play. When we surrender control, we open ourselves up to peace and guidance that surpasses our understanding. So, when things get overwhelming today, remember to loosen your grip and let God steer.

PRAYER

Heavenly Father, I surrender my worries and fears to You. Help me to let go of control and trust in Your plan. Fill me with peace and guide me with Your wisdom. When I am anxious and overwhelmed, remind me of Your love and Your promises. Teach me to rest in Your care and to trust that You are working all things for my good. Give me the courage to release my grip and to follow Your lead with faith. Let Your peace guard my heart and mind, and let Your Spirit guide me in all things. In Jesus' name, Amen.

"Cast your cares on the Lord and he will sustain you; he will never let the righteous be shaken."
Psalm 55:22

QUESTIONS TO REFLECT ON

1. What worries or fears do you need to release to God's care?
2. How can letting go and trusting God change your outlook on difficult situations?

notes

_____

_____

_____

_____

_____

_____

_____

Day 18

HAVING HOPE IN UNCERTAINTY

In times of uncertainty, it's easy to feel lost and overwhelmed, but holding on to hope can be our anchor. Hope isn't just wishful thinking; it's a confident expectation that something good is on the horizon, even if we can't see it yet. When life feels out of control, remember that there's a greater plan at work. Trusting in this can bring peace to our hearts and strength to our spirits. Like a seed planted in the dark soil, our hope can grow and blossom in ways we never imagined, bringing light to even our darkest days. So, let's hold onto hope, believing that each step forward, no matter how small, is leading us to brighter days ahead.

PRAYER

Heavenly Father, in the midst of uncertainty, I seek Your peace and reassurance. When life feels chaotic and unpredictable, remind me that You are my steadfast anchor. Help me to place my hope in You, knowing that You are in control of all things. Fill me with Your presence and give me the strength to face each day with confidence in Your plans. Teach me to trust in Your unfailing love and to find comfort in Your promises. When I am overwhelmed with doubt or fear, calm my heart and mind with Your peace. Guide me to lean on You and to find hope in Your Word, knowing that You are always working for my good. Let my hope be a light to others, reflecting Your faithfulness and grace in every situation. In Jesus' name, Amen.

"May the God of hope fill you with all joy and peace as you
trust in him, so that you may overflow with hope by the
power of the Holy Spirit."
Romans 15:13

QUESTIONS TO REFLECT ON

1. What are some current uncertainties in your life where you need
to place your hope in God?
2. How can you cultivate a mindset of hope and trust in God's
plan during uncertain times?

notes

Leaning on God

God has taught me that you never need to worry about tomorrow. You survived yesterday. You are alive and dealing with today. With God's help, you can face tomorrow and whatever may come your way.

JESUS LOVES YOU

It's easy to forget that amidst all our imperfections, Jesus loves us unconditionally. His love isn't contingent on our successes or failures; it's a constant, unwavering presence. Imagine a love that sees beyond our flaws, forgives our mistakes, and embraces us in our entirety. Jesus' love is like that—a comforting assurance that we are cherished just as we are. It's a profound reminder that we don't need to earn this love; we simply need to accept it, allowing it to transform our lives and radiate through our actions toward others. So, take a moment today to feel the warmth of Jesus' love, knowing that you are valued and embraced in the arms of a love that surpasses understanding.

PRAYER

Jesus, thank You for Your incredible love. Help me to feel Your presence and to know that I am deeply loved by You. Let Your love transform my heart and guide my actions today. Teach me to love others as You have loved me, and to show Your kindness and grace in all that I do. When I feel unloved or unworthy, remind me of the depth of Your love and the sacrifice You made for me. Fill me with Your love so that I can share it with the world around me. Let my life be a reflection of Your love and a testimony to Your grace. In Jesus' name, Amen.

BIBLE VERSE

"See what great love the Father has lavished on us, that we should be called children of God! And that is what we are! The reason the world does not know us is that it did not know him."
1 John 3:1

QUESTIONS TO REFLECT ON

1. How do you experience Jesus' love in your daily life?
2. How can you share the love of Jesus with others today?

notes

_____

_____

_____

_____

_____

_____

_____

Day 20

TRANSFORMED BY GOD'S GRACE

In the midst of life's twists and turns, find solace in the realization that God has been at work, molding and shaping you. We need to thank Him for the profound changes He has brought about – the healing, the growth, and the strength to overcome. In moments of self-reflection, we see the fingerprints of His touch, guiding us toward a better version of ourselves. Today, as you offer thanks, acknowledge that this journey of change is ongoing, and trust that God's transformative love will continue to shape you into the individual He intends you to be.

PRAYER

Lord, Your grace is amazing and transformative. Change me from the inside out and help me to reflect Your love and mercy. Teach me to extend Your grace to others and live a life that honors You. When I stumble and fall, remind me of Your forgiveness and Your power to make all things new. Help me to grow in Your grace and to become more like Jesus each day. Let Your grace be evident in my words, actions, and attitudes. Fill me with Your Spirit and guide me to live a life that brings glory to Your name.
In Jesus' name, Amen.

BIBLE VERSE

"Therefore, if anyone is in Christ, the new creation has come:
The old has gone, the new is here!"
2 Corinthians 5:17

QUESTIONS TO REFLECT ON

1. How has God's grace transformed you in the past?
2. In what areas of your life do you need to experience more of God's grace?

notes

_____

_____

_____

_____

_____

_____

_____

STANDING ON TRUTH

Honesty stands as a guiding light, while deceit casts shadows that can darken our path. The dangers of lying extend beyond the immediate consequences; they corrode trust, sow seeds of discord, and erode the foundation of meaningful relationships. A lie, like a subtle poison, may offer a momentary escape, but it leaves a lasting stain on our character. As we navigate life's twists and turns, remember that honesty not only fosters authenticity but also builds bridges of trust that withstand the tests of time. Embracing truth becomes a steadfast companion, guiding us toward a life rooted in integrity and genuine connections.

PRAYER

Father, help me to stand firm in Your truth. When the world around me is uncertain, remind me of Your unchanging Word. Give me the courage to live out my faith boldly and share Your truth with others. Teach me to discern truth from falsehood and to hold fast to Your promises. When I face opposition or doubt, strengthen my resolve and fill me with Your peace. Let Your truth be the foundation of my life, guiding my decisions and shaping my character. Help me to be a light in the darkness, sharing Your truth with love and grace. In Jesus' name, Amen.

"The Lord detests lying lips, but he delights in people who are trustworthy."
Proverbs 12:22

QUESTIONS TO REFLECT ON

1. What truths from God's Word do you need to stand on today?
2. How can holding onto God's truth help you in challenging times?

notes

_____

_____

_____

_____

_____

_____

_____

Trust God With What's Ahead

You can't always see where the road leads,
but God promises there's something better
up ahead. You just have to trust Him.

JESUS IS ENOUGH

Sometimes we feel like we need a lot of things to make us happy or fulfilled, like success, money, or popularity. But Jesus teaches us that He alone is enough. When we have Jesus in our lives, we have everything we need. His love, grace, and presence are sufficient to satisfy our deepest longings and to give us true joy and peace. So, let's trust in Jesus and find our contentment in Him, knowing that He is always enough for us.

PRAYER

Lord, remind me that You are enough. When I feel lacking or incomplete, help me to find my sufficiency in You. Fill me with Your presence and let Your love be my greatest treasure. Teach me to seek You above all else and to trust that You provide everything I need. When I am tempted to look for fulfillment in other places, draw me back to You. Let my heart be satisfied in Your love and let my life reflect the joy and peace that comes from knowing You. In Jesus' name, Amen.

"But he said to me, 'My grace is sufficient for you, for my power is made perfect in weakness.' Therefore I will boast all the more gladly about my weaknesses, so that Christ's power may rest on me."
2 Corinthians 12:9

QUESTIONS TO REFLECT ON

1. In what areas of your life do you need to remind yourself that Jesus is enough?
2. How can finding sufficiency in Jesus bring you peace and contentment?

notes

_____

_____

_____

_____

_____

_____

_____

THE CHANGING OF SEASONS

Just as the seasons change in nature, so too does God bring different seasons into our lives. Sometimes we experience the warmth and growth of Spring, filled with new beginnings and opportunities. Other times, we face the challenges and transitions of Autumn, where things may feel like they're falling away. In every season, God's hand is guiding us, teaching us, and preparing us for what's to come. Even in the cold of Winter, when everything seems dormant, God is working behind the scenes, orchestrating our growth and renewal. Trusting in God's timing and purpose, we can find peace and strength in every season of our lives.

PRAYER

Father, as the seasons change, remind me of Your constant presence. Help me to embrace the new opportunities and challenges each season brings, trusting that You are with me through it all. Teach me to see Your hand in every season of life and to find joy in the journey. When I face difficult transitions, give me the strength to adapt and the faith to trust in Your plan. Let my life be a reflection of Your faithfulness and a testimony to Your unchanging love. Guide me through each season with grace and wisdom.
In Jesus' name, Amen.

BIBLE VERSE

"There is a time for everything, and a season for every activity under the heavens..."
Ecclesiastes 3:1

QUESTIONS TO REFLECT ON

1. How can you see God's hand in the changing seasons of your life?
1. What can you learn from the current season you are in?

notes

Day 24

GLORIFYING GOD THROUGH ACTIONS

Doing what brings glory to God means living in a way that reflects His character and honors His name. It's about loving others, being kind, showing compassion, and living with integrity. When we strive to live in a way that pleases God, we not only bring Him glory but also experience true fulfillment and purpose in our own lives. So, whether it's through our actions, words, or attitudes, let's seek to glorify God in everything we do, knowing that He is pleased when we live in alignment with His will.

PRAYER

Lord, help me to glorify You in everything I do. Let my actions reflect Your love and bring honor to Your name. Give me the strength and wisdom to live in a way that points others to You. Teach me to seek Your glory above all else and to serve others with humility and grace. When I am tempted to seek my own recognition, remind me that my purpose is to honor You. Let my life be a beacon of Your love, showing the world the beauty of a life lived for You. In Jesus' name, Amen.

BIBLE VERSE

"And whatever you do, whether in word or deed, do it all in the name of the Lord Jesus, giving thanks to God the Father through him."
Colossians 3:17

QUESTIONS TO REFLECT ON

1. What actions can you take today to glorify God in your life?
2. How can your behavior reflect God's love to those around you?

notes

_____

_____

_____

_____

_____

_____

_____

Trust God Everyday

God created a way for you last time and
He will create one this time. Whatever you
are worrying about, He has a plan. He is
bigger than your fears. He is stronger than
the obstacles in front of you. He is with
you. Have faith and trust Him.

NOTHING IS IMPOSSIBLE
WITH GOD

No matter how big or daunting our challenges may seem, we can find comfort in knowing that nothing is impossible for God. When we feel overwhelmed or uncertain, we can turn to Him with faith, knowing that His power surpasses all limitations. In moments of doubt, let's remember that God is capable of moving mountains, guiding us through even the toughest of circumstances. With trust in His unfailing love and strength, we can face any obstacle knowing that He is with us, making the impossible possible.

PRAYER

Heavenly Father, remind me that nothing is impossible for You. When I face challenges, help me to trust in Your power and believe in Your miracles. Strengthen my faith and give me hope in the impossible. Teach me to pray with boldness and to expect great things from You. When I am discouraged, remind me of Your mighty works and Your unfailing promises. Let my life be a testimony to Your greatness and Your ability to do the impossible. Fill me with Your Spirit and guide me to live with confident faith. In Jesus' name, Amen.

BIBLE VERSE

"I am the Lord , the God of all mankind. Is anything too hard for me?"
Jeremiah 32:27

QUESTIONS TO REFLECT ON

1. What impossible situation are you facing that you need to trust God with?
2. How can remembering God's power and past miracles strengthen your faith?

notes

_____

_____

_____

_____

_____

_____

_____

BEING IN AWE OF GOD

When I pause to reflect on the beauty that surrounds me, I can't help but feel a profound awe for God. It's in the intricate details of nature, the warmth of relationships, and the gentle whispers of hope that I see His hand at work. The Creator of the universe, who shaped galaxies and painted sunsets, is also intimately involved in the creation of my existence. This awe isn't born out of fear but from a deep sense of gratitude and wonder, realizing that I am known and loved by a God whose power and goodness are bigger than my understanding. In awe, I find solace, inspiration, and a reminder that there's something infinitely greater than myself at the heart of this incredible journey called life.

PRAYER

Lord, open my eyes to the wonder of Your creation and Your mighty works. Fill me with awe and reverence for who You are. Help me to worship You with a heart full of gratitude and praise. Teach me to see Your hand in the beauty of the world around me and in the blessings of my life. When I am tempted to take things for granted, remind me of Your greatness and Your love. Let my life be a continual act of worship, reflecting my awe and reverence for You. Guide me to live with a sense of wonder and a heart full of praise. In Jesus' name, Amen.

"The heavens declare the glory of God; the skies proclaim the work of his hands."
Psalm 19:1

QUESTIONS TO REFLECT ON

1. What aspects of God's creation or character fill you with awe?
2. How can living in awe of God change your daily perspective?

notes

LISTENING TO GOD'S VOICE

It's crucial to tune our hearts to hear the voice of God amidst the noise of the world. Just as a shepherd knows the distinct call of each of their sheep, so too does God speak uniquely to each of us. However, amidst the chaos of life, the enemy seeks to sow confusion and doubt, whispering lies to lead us astray. Yet, by immersing ourselves in prayer, Scripture, and quiet reflection, we can hear the gentle whisper of God's truth, guiding us towards love, peace, and purpose. Let us be vigilant in listening to God's voice today, for it alone leads us to abundant life and eternal joy.

PRAYER

Father, help me to hear Your voice in the midst of life's noise. Quiet my heart and mind so I can listen to Your guidance. Lead me on the right path and give me the courage to follow Your direction. Teach me to discern Your voice from all others and to trust in Your wisdom. When I am uncertain, remind me to seek You in prayer and to listen for Your still, small voice. Let Your Spirit guide me and fill me with peace and clarity. Help me to live in obedience to Your will, trusting that You are always leading me. In Jesus' name, Amen.

"My sheep listen to my voice; I know them, and they follow me."
John 10:27

QUESTIONS TO REFLECT ON

1. How can you create a quiet space to listen for God's voice in your life?
2. What steps can you take to better discern God's guidance?

notes

God Always Responds

It's not that God is silent, it's that
the world is noisy.

Sometimes God answers with
a whisper to see it we are
paying attention.

FINDING A GODLY SPOUSE

Marrying someone who brings you closer to God is like finding a precious gem in a vast desert. It's a union where love isn't just about companionship but also about spiritual growth. Together, you journey through a life together, supporting and uplifting each other through life's highs and lows. In their presence, you find solace, strength, and a deeper understanding of your faith. It's a partnership blessed by God, where love becomes a sacred path towards Him.

PRAYER

Lord, I pray for a spouse who loves You above all else. Guide me to someone who will encourage my faith and walk with me in Your ways. Help me to trust in Your timing and Your perfect plan for my life. Teach me to become the person You want me to be, preparing me for a godly relationship. When I feel lonely or impatient, remind me of Your love and Your promises. Fill me with hope and faith, knowing that You are working all things for my good. Let my future marriage be a reflection of Your love and a testimony to Your faithfulness. In Jesus' name, Amen.

"Two are better than one, because they have a good return for their labor: If either of them falls down, one can help the other up. But pity anyone who falls and has no one to help them up."
Ecclesiastes 4:9-10

QUESTIONS TO REFLECT ON

1. What qualities are you praying for in a godly spouse?
2. How can you prepare yourself to be a godly partner?

notes

_____

_____

_____

_____

_____

_____

_____

Day 29

DISCOVERING FAITH AMID CHAOS

Where chaos reigns and uncertainty looms, our faith becomes the anchor that steadies our souls. Like a ship navigating rough waters, we are called to trust in the unwavering guidance of our Creator. Surrender your understanding to God's wisdom, embracing His path as the surest route through the mess of life. Amidst the noise of the world, let us quiet our hearts, leaning not on our own understanding but on the promise that God will lead us through. When chaos and worldly noise overwhelms you, may your faith be the beacon that guides you to calmer shores, and may you find peace in the knowledge that you are held in the loving hands of our Heavenly Father.

PRAYER

Heavenly Father, in the chaos of life, help me to find faith. Strengthen my trust in You and give me peace in the storm. Remind me that You are in control and that Your love never fails. Teach me to lean on You when everything around me feels uncertain. Fill me with Your peace that surpasses all understanding, and help me to rest in Your promises. Let my faith be a light in the darkness, guiding me through the chaos with confidence in Your sovereignty. In Jesus' name, Amen.

BIBLE VERSE

"So do not fear, for I am with you; do not be dismayed, for I am your God. I will strengthen you and help you; I will uphold you with my righteous right hand."
Isaiah 41:10

QUESTIONS TO REFLECT ON

1. How can you find moments of peace and faith in the midst of chaos?
2. What Bible verses or promises can you hold onto during uncertain times?

notes

_____

_____

_____

_____

_____

_____

_____

STEP OUT IN FAITH EACH DAY

Every morning is like standing at the edge of a cliff, unsure of what lies ahead. But instead of fear, let faith be your wings. Take that step, even if it feels like a leap into the unknown. Believe that as you face the day with courage and trust, you'll be upheld by unseen hands. Just like a bird takes flight with confidence, let your faith lift you higher, knowing that with each step, you're closer to fulfilling your purpose and experiencing the beauty of God's plan for your life.

PRAYER

Lord, give me the courage to step out in faith each day. Help me to trust You with my decisions and to follow Your lead. Fill me with boldness and confidence in Your promises. Teach me to rely on Your strength and to walk in obedience to Your will. When I am afraid or uncertain, remind me of Your faithfulness and Your power. Let my life be a testimony of Your goodness and Your ability to guide me in all things. Help me to live each day with faith, trusting that You are always with me. In Jesus' name, Amen.

"Now faith is confidence in what we hope for and assurance about what we do not see."
Hebrews 11:1

QUESTIONS TO REFLECT ON

1. What steps of faith is God calling you to take today?
2. How can you remind yourself to trust God as you step out in faith daily?

notes

_____

_____

_____

_____

_____

_____

_____

Relax and Trust God

I don't know who needs to read this but
Isaiah 60:22 says "When the time is
right, I the Lord will make it happen."

So, relax and trust God today.

About The Author

In 2014, Kevin Jackson founded Living Christian, a global online ministry dedicated to helping Christians and families thrive. Living Christian provides resources for Christians to live by their faith 7 days a week and for parents to raise their children according to the values grounded in biblical principles.

Kevin is a successful writer, blogger, and social media personality. He also currently hosts the popular bi-weekly podcast series "Bible Reading and Coffee Drinking".

His debut children's book, "Bear Goes Home For Christmas," is a heartwarming tale that speaks to the essence of the holiday season. Through his writing, Kevin invites readers to explore the intersection of faith and everyday life, offering hope in a complex and fallen world.

With a blend of compassion and creativity, he continues to inspire and uplift audiences worldwide. Whether through LivingChristian.org, or his various blogs and social posts, Kevin remains dedicated to spreading messages of love, faith, and encouragement to everyone that he encounters.

Kevin and his wonderful wife, along with their two beautiful daughters, two dogs, and a cat who believes he's a dog, reside outside of Austin, Texas.

You can learn more at www.UpSlant.com
or www.LivingChristian.org.

Made in the USA
Columbia, SC
04 October 2024

43648906R00050